THE
CORPORAL WORKS
of Mommy
    (and Daddy Too!)

THE
CORPORAL WORKS
of Mommy
(and Daddy Too!)

– Dr. Greg and Lisa Popcak –

Our Sunday Visitor

www.osv.com
Our Sunday Visitor Publishing Division
Our Sunday Visitor, Inc.
Huntington, Indiana 46750

Nihil Obstat
Msgr. Michael Heintz, Ph.D.
Censor Librorum

Imprimatur
✠ Kevin C. Rhoades
Bishop of Fort Wayne-South Bend
February 20, 2016

The *Nihil Obstat* and *Imprimatur* are official declarations that a book is free from doctrinal or moral error. It is not implied that those who have granted the *Nihil Obstat* and *Imprimatur* agree with the contents, opinions, or statements expressed.

Every reasonable effort has been made to determine copyright holders of excerpted materials and to secure permissions as needed. If any copyrighted materials have been inadvertently used in this work without proper credit being given in one form or another, please notify Our Sunday Visitor in writing so that future printings of this work may be corrected accordingly.

Our Sunday Visitor Publishing Division, Our Sunday Visitor, Inc., 200 Noll Plaza, Huntington, IN 46750; 1-800-348-2440

ISBN: 978-1-68192-033-7 (Inventory No. T1787)
eISBN: 978-1-68192-034-4
LCCN: 2016933961

Cover design: Amanda Falk
Cover art: Shutterstock
Interior design: Dianne Nelson

PRINTED IN THE UNITED STATES OF AMERICA

Table of Contents

CHAPTER ONE

Introduction

In the Sermon on the Mount, Jesus says, "Blessed are the merciful, for they will be shown mercy" (Mt 5:6). As Pope Francis has reminded us, mercy is a defining virtue of the Christian walk. What does it mean to be merciful? And what difference does it make in the life of your family?

If you consider both the **corporal works of mercy** — for example, give food to the hungry, give drink to the thirsty, shelter the homeless, etc. — and the **spiritual works of mercy** altogether, it becomes clear that "being merciful" means *treating others in a manner that allows them to see their profound worth in God's eyes.* Is there a more important, or more opportune, place to practice this than in the heart of your family's home?

Each Person Is Sacred
The United States Conference of Catholic Bishops once asserted that each person "must be re-

spected with a reverence that is religious. When we deal with each other, we should do so with the sense of awe that arises in the presence of something holy and sacred. For that is what human beings are: we are created in the image of God" (*Economic Justice for All*, 28).

When we show mercy to others — especially by living out the various works of mercy — we remind each other that no matter what we look like, no matter what our station in life, and no matter what we have done, we are sacred and precious in God's sight.

We'll Always Be Royals

A popular song by singer Lorde proclaims, "We'll never be royals." Christians know that nothing could be further from the truth! Each person is made in God's image and likeness. Baptism enables us to be prophets, priests, *and royals*. As the *Catechism of the Catholic Church* puts it:

> The People of God shares in the *royal* office of Christ. He exercises his kingship by drawing all men to himself through his death and Resurrection. Christ, King and

Lord of the universe, made himself the servant of all, for he came "not to be served but to serve, and to give his life as a ransom for many" [Mt 20:28]. For the Christian, "to reign is to serve him," particularly when serving "the poor and the suffering, in whom the Church recognizes the image of her poor and suffering founder" [*Lumen Gentium* 8; cf. 36]. The People of God fulfills its royal dignity by a life in keeping with its vocation to serve with Christ. (786)

But it's important to remember why we attend to others' physical needs. In his Theology of the Body, Pope St. John Paul II famously asserted that "the body and it alone, is capable of making visible what is invisible: the spiritual and the divine" (General Audience, February 20, 1980). In other words, when we practice the works of mercy, we aren't just caring for each other's bodies; we celebrate each other's dignity as persons and assert that each of us is an heir to the kingdom of God — destined, through God's merciful grace, to reign with him forever.

We engage in works of mercy such as *clothing*

the naked because every child of God deserves to be dressed in a manner that reveals his or her dignity as a son or daughter of the King of Kings! We *feed the hungry* because every person deserves to know he or she has a rightful place at the royal feast set at God's table! We *forgive willingly* and *bear wrongs patiently* because we recognize the challenges involved in becoming saints, and we try to be generous about the struggle that's part of that process. And yet, when those we love forget who they really are, neglecting to strive for greatness and, instead, deciding to wallow in their brokenness, we *admonish the sinner*, not to condemn or judge but to invite them to remember that they were meant to be more, and to live more fully than they are.

Mercy: The Heart of the Home

Many families mistakenly think that the ways they care for one another at home somehow don't count and that the works of mercy are something missionaries practice when ministering to the poor in far-off lands. In truth, most people's biggest opportunity to practice mercy — and, in particular, the works of mercy — *is right at home!* The Church has long taught that the family is a *school of human-*

ity: a place where children and adults together discover their value as persons by the way they love, respect, and care for one another. It's because of this critical role that family life is ground zero for learning to walk the way of mercy. Any authentic expressions of mercy we carry out in the world must be rooted in the lessons of mercy we learn in the home. Christian parents and children work to help each other discover their worth in God's eyes in the little interactions they share throughout the day. The way we families eat, drink, dress, keep our homes, and all the rest are not merely ways we attend to our bodily needs; they are ways we proclaim to each other, "You are a child of God!"

The Corporal Works of Mommy and Daddy & The "Little Way" of the Family

When our oldest child was preparing for his first Communion, we were reviewing the various works of mercy. When he heard that they included things like *feeding the hungry, giving drink to the thirsty,* and *clothing the naked,* he looked up at us and said: "You guys do those things all the time. They should call them the corporal works of mommy — and daddy too!"

In his innocent exuberance, our son stumbled upon a great spiritual truth. St. Thérèse of Lisieux promoted what she called the "little way of holiness" — the idea that every person could achieve great heights of holiness by doing small acts with great love. The works of mercy as practiced at home — what we have come to call "the corporal works of mommy and daddy" — remind us that charity truly does begin at home, and more often than not, there is no better place to remind one another what we are worth in God's eyes — that is, to practice mercy — than in the home.

In this book, you'll discover the multitude of little ways God wants to use the simple daily activities of your family life to remind you of your worth in his eyes and empower you to fulfill his destiny as his very own sons and daughters. The following is a taste of what you'll uncover.

The Corporal Works of Mommy and Daddy: An Overview

Feed the Hungry: Family members truly bless one another when they create a nurturing place around the dinner table for communion and conversation to occur and when they take time to plan nourishing, heartwarming meals. Considerable research reveals the benefits of families sitting down to meals together, including everything from better physical and mental health outcomes to higher academic achievement and greater life and relationship satisfaction. Add "growing in holiness" to the list!

Give Drink to the Thirsty: What parent hasn't been asked to get a thirsty child a drink in the middle of the night? Getting up and serving that child cheerfully with compassion is a work of mercy that reminds the child that his or her needs are important and that he or she will be heard and loved even when it is inconvenient for us to do so.

Clothe the Naked: Finding the grace to be patient while dealing with a toddler who only wants to wear the blue shirt or helping a teen dress attractively yet modestly isn't just an exercise in patience; it's an opportunity to help your children remember their worth in God's eyes!

Shelter the Homeless: Putting in the thought, time, and effort it takes to make your house a welcoming home by working to make it a beautiful and orderly, yet comfortable and hospitable, place is a great way to remind yourself and your family of your dignity as children of God. And teaching your family to be good stewards of what you have been given is an important lesson in godly gratitude.

Visit the Sick: When you respond lovingly to a sick child, refusing to treat him or her as a burden or an inconvenience even though the illness has thrown your schedule into chaos, you are practicing mercy, growing in personal holiness, and showing your child his or her worth in God's eyes and yours.

Visit the Imprisoned: It is one thing to banish our children to their rooms or to a timeout when they have committed some offense, but when we visit them a few minutes later, talk them through their error, teach them what to do instead, and work to heal their hurts and rebuild our relationship, we are practicing true mercy and showing our children they still have worth in God's eyes and our eyes, even when they mess up.

Bury the Dead: Helping a child deal with sad transitions in life, whether due to the loss of a pet or favorite relative or other events that can turn family life upside down, requires incredible compassion and sensitivity, especially when we are dealing with our own grief. Doing this well enables our children to connect with God's loving presence even in times of sadness.

The Spiritual Works of Mommy and Daddy

Of course, there are *spiritual* works of mommy and daddy, too. There isn't room to address these in this book, but viewed through the lens of the little way of family life, it should be obvious that there are ample opportunities to admonish wrongdoing, instruct each other in the right things to do, help each other work through doubts, comfort each other in times of sadness, bear wrongs patiently, forgive willingly, and pray for one another.

Saint-Making Machines

Clearly, our homes can become saint-making machines if we simply realize the transforming, spiritual power that exists behind even the most mundane tasks of family life. We can use the corporal works of mommy and daddy to cooperate with God's plan to make us and our children into the saints we were created to be!

God has incredible plans for your family! May those plans unfold in your home as you explore all of the ways the corporal works of mommy and daddy can help you experience the family life God wants for you!

CHAPTER TWO

Feed the Hungry

So Jesus said to them, "Amen, amen, I say to you, it was not Moses who gave the bread from heaven; my Father gives you the true bread from heaven. For the bread of God is that which comes down from heaven and gives life to the world." So they said to him, "Sir, give us this bread always." Jesus said to them, "I am the bread of life; whoever comes to me will never hunger."

John 6:32-35

Feeding your family can seem like the height of drudgery. As one mom we know jokingly put it: "They want to eat ... again? I just fed them yesterday!"

At first blush it can be hard to imagine that feeding your family could possibly be a spiritual exercise, but when you really think about it, it is hard to imagine an activity that bears more fruit than having regular family meals. God himself models the importance of family mealtime. He takes time out of the busiest schedule in the universe to sit down each day with his children at the family meal that is the Eucharist. The Eucharist is a profound sign that food feeds not only the body but the soul as well.

Ongoing research asserts that the simple ritual of regular family mealtimes is directly connected to happier marriage and family lives, increased physical and mental well-being for parents and children, better academic performance for students, and better behavior for both children and adolescents.

If family life is, as the Church asserts, a school of humanity, the family table is the place that the majority of those lessons are taught. The corporal work of mercy exhorting us to *feed the hungry* reminds us that family mealtimes don't just feed our bellies. Like the Eucharist, they feed our souls as well.

Family meals are a great opportunity to grow in holiness. St. Catherine of Siena was known throughout the world for her wisdom, courage, and holy visions, but the thing that impressed St. Francis de Sales most about her was how she used the simple tasks of everyday life to grow closer to God. When she made dinner, she used to imagine cooking for Jesus. When she brought the food to the table, she would imagine that she was serving the apostles. This simple meditation enabled St. Catherine to turn feeding the hungry people in her house into a spiritual exercise, and the holiness and wisdom she gained from performing these simple acts with great love, in part, led to her being honored as a Doctor of the Church. In fact, St. Francis de Sales asserted that it was the holiness with which she attended to these tasks that prepared her to enter into the deeper mystical experiences for which she became famous. Her willingness to find the sacred in the mundane enabled her to encounter the sacred face-to-face.

Here are some ways you can begin to walk the little way of family life by practicing *feed the hungry* as a corporal work of mommy and daddy.

1. Ask Yourself: Who Is This For?

Take a page from St Catherine of Siena's book and ask yourself, "For whom am I doing this?" Imagine that you are preparing meals for the Lord and

serving his apostles at table. That doesn't mean that
you have to put on spiritual airs or speak any differently with your spouse and kids than you nor-
mally would. It just means realizing that "whatever
you did for one of these least brothers of mine,
you did for me" (Mt 25:40) and giving this simple
task of meal preparation the attention it deserves.

2. Cooking with the Saints

When you're making a meal, especially if you're
trying a new recipe and worried about getting it
right (or how it might be received), take a moment to ask the saints to cook with you! We like
to ask for the Blessed Mother's intercession especially: "Blessed Mother, help us to prepare a meal
worthy of your family. Ask Our Lord to let this
food be good, nourishing, and enjoyable, and an
opportunity for us to draw closer to God and each
other." By all means, use your own words. Regardless of what you pray or what saint's intercession you invoke, such a simple prayer can help you
connect deeper spiritual meaning with each meal
you make!

3. Pray a Meaningful Grace Before Meals

A recent survey by CARA (the Center for Applied Research in the Apostolate) shows that only 13 percent of Catholic families consistently say grace before meals, yet this is one of the easiest ways to begin cultivating a habit for family prayer. The most common form of grace before meals is "Bless us, O Lord, and these your gifts, which we are about to receive from your bounty, through Christ Our Lord. Amen." Saying this simple prayer *thoughtfully* can fill your mealtimes with meaning.

But don't stop there! Take a moment in prayer together to recount the blessings of the day and lift up any special concerns. Ultimately, prayer should draw your family closer to God *and* one another. Prayer is ultimately about intimacy — learning about each other's joys, concerns, and aspirations, and then bringing those things to God so that he might bless, comfort, and counsel you. Make the most of mealtimes so that they feed your souls as well as your bellies!

4. Don't Just Eat, Talk!

Part of making mealtimes a sacred space is making sure to use these times to share a little bit about your lives. Don't accept "I don't know" and "Nothing" as answers to "What did you do today?" These phrases are a strategy kids use to see if you really care to know. Push back a little by asking *specific* questions: "I know you were struggling with long division in math yesterday. How'd that go in class today?" "You said you were getting together with the team to do drills today. What happened?" Specific questions mean, "I care enough to know what to ask."

Make conversation possible by turning off the television and putting away smartphones and other devices. Even in those instances where "family dinner" is a quick burger in the car between games, turn off the radio, put away the smartphones, say grace, and talk to each other! It is your presence, and your willingness to invite God to your meal, that makes the moment sacred.

Don't be afraid to take your mealtime conversations to the next level by initiating conversations about each other's thoughts, feelings, and the ways God is moving in your lives. If you don't know how to do this, a quick Google search of "conversation cards" will yield an abundance of resources.

These cards feature simple questions of the day that can take your conversations in fun and surprising directions. Use them as a springboard for more meaningful family discussions. As we point out in *Discovering God Together: The Catholic Guide to Raising Faithful Kids*, research consistently shows that children are more likely to own their faith as adults when *they experience their faith as the source of the warmth in their homes*. Mealtimes that begin with prayer and continue with family sharing create the warmth that makes faith and values stick.

5. Cook Together

Besides eating together, cooking together can also be a great way to turn feeding the hungry people in your home into a spiritual exercise. Cooking together encourages the spirit of generous mutual service — what Pope St. John Paul II referred to as "mutual self-donation" — that healthy family life depends upon. Families that work together learn to trust one another, to be generous to one another, and take ownership in the tasks that are part and parcel of creating a home. Make sure mom and dad, sisters and brothers, all pitch in on a regular basis to help make the meals, get the meals to the table, and clean up together afterward. Don't just treat these things as a chore. Let them be a family activity that draw you closer together and help you learn from one another.

6. Meal Planning

There are many resources for meal planning, but many of these simply focus on the mechanics of getting a healthy rotation of nutritious foods to the table. When doing your own meal plan, remember that connection is as important as nutrition. In fact, planning a week of meals or more before food shopping helps the person who has to get the meals on the table stay in a calmer mood, and be more present to the family, come the chaos of the dinner hour. Keep your relationship in mind when meal planning. On less busy days, discuss, as a family, how you might make that mealtime a little more special. Perhaps there are some favorite meals the family might enjoy. Can you cook them together? On busier days, don't overwhelm yourself. A simpler meal that allows you time and energy to talk and share is better than a perfect meal that leaves you spent and irritable.

7. *Don't Fight about Food*

Generosity and self-control are important virtues, but they're easily squelched by arguments about food. Make a rule that while family members can express preferences for the foods they are served, they may not complain about what they are served. Complaining undermines gratitude and makes mealtime seem like something to be survived. A pleasant, grateful spirit must be the price of admission to the family table. Pouters and complainers may stay in their rooms until they can get themselves in a more generous frame of mind.

Mealtime is also a great opportunity for parents to grow in virtue as we learn to gracefully manage our children's eating habits. Encouraging a grateful spirit at the family table doesn't require parents to turn mealtimes into power struggles. Small tummies mean small portions. Better to give children less and have them ask for more than give them too much and create both tension and waste.

If your children don't finish what you feel is an age-appropriate serving, don't force them to sit until the plate is clean. Simply wrap it up and save it for later when they are hungry again. When your child turns his or her nose up at new foods, don't

force the child to eat it all, but do require that he
or she eat at least one mouthful before leaving the
table. Don't let the child off the hook, but be pleasant about it. Gentle, consistent encouragement allows both appetites and palettes grow with time.
We offer more dinnertime discipline ideas in our
book *Parenting with Grace*, but the most important
takeaway is to not concern yourself so much about
making children eat as with facilitating the kind
of relationship that will make them more willing
to try new things as they mature. Throughout this
process moms and dads will be invited to grow in
patience and compassion, and their children will
be encouraged to grow in gratitude, self-control,
and openness.

8. Share What You Have

Through the works of mercy, Christian families
have a wonderful opportunity not only to walk
the little way of family life at home but also to
live their Christian mission in the world as well.
Teach your children the value of sharing what you
have. For instance, at least once a month, make a
double batch of an easily frozen meal as a family.
Your family can enjoy the first batch, but take the

other to someone you know who is sick or had a new baby. Let your pastor know that you are willing to provide meals for those families who are going through a difficult time.

Do you notice that you throw away a lot of groceries? According to the Natural Resources Defense Council, about 40 percent of edible food in the United States ends up being thrown away. Think about buying less food at the store and donate the difference you spend to a local food bank.

These are just a few ways feeding the hungry in your home can become an opportunity to grow closer to God and cooperate with his grace to become the family he wants you to be. Consider the following questions to help draw more spiritual growth out of feeding the hungry in your home as a corporal work of mommy and daddy.

– QUESTIONS FOR REFLECTION –

- When do you most enjoy eating together as a family? How could you make these enjoyable mealtimes happen more often?
- Do you pray at meals? What could you do to make mealtime prayer more meaningful?

- Is your family practicing generous service by working together on meal preparation and cleanup? What could you do to take even better advantage of this time to draw closer together by working closer together around food prep?
- Do you enjoy the conversations that go on around your family table? What things can you do to make mealtime conversations more meaningful?
- What are ways you, as a family, can be more conscious of those families without enough to eat? What simple things could you do each month as a family to help feed the hungry in your community?
- Sit down as a family and discuss the following: What other ways can you make giving food to the hungry a spiritual exercise that blesses your home and community? Write them in the space below.

Prayer

Lord Jesus Christ, You give us yourself as the Living Bread so that we might never be hungry for you. Help us to approach mealtimes in a way that feeds our souls as well as our bodies and satisfies our hunger for connection as a family as much as our hunger for food. Let our mealtimes be times of cooperation, gratitude, service, friendship, and fellowship. And help us to see the opportunities for spiritual growth contained within feeding the hungry in our home. Amen.

CHAPTER THREE

Give Drink to the Thirsty

Jesus answered and said to her, "Everyone who drinks of this water will be thirsty again; but whoever drinks the water I shall give will never thirst; the water that I shall give will become in him a spring of water welling up to eternal life." The woman said to him, "Sir, give me this water, so that I may not be thirsty."

John 4:13-15

When Jesus was at the well with the Samaritan woman, he recognized that she was not just thirsting for water. She was thirsting for innocence, for meaning, for purpose, for intimacy, and for connection with God. He satisfied her thirst not only with the fresh water created by the Father and drawn from Jacob's well, but also with the Living Water that flowed from his heart of love, a love that confirmed her dignity and worth as a child of God.

Giving drink to the thirsty while walking the little way of family life means knowing what your family is thirsting for. Time? Attention? Affection? Peace? God? How are you meeting these needs? What more can you do to more adequately respond to this thirst?

As you saw in the chapter on feeding the hungry, the difference between simply meeting a physical need and performing a corporal work of mommy and daddy is a willingness to see the need behind the need, a desire to attend to the spiritual longing — no matter how simple — that is often hidden behind the expression of a physical need.

Is the child who asks for a drink of water in the middle of the night really just thirsty for a glass of water, or are they thirsting for a little comfort? When you bring a glass of lemonade to a spouse or child who is dripping with sweat from working in the garden, are they really just grateful for the hydration? Or are they thirsting for your appreciation? When you ask a friend out for a drink, are you really just relishing the opportunity for liquid refreshment? Or are you thirsting for connection? In each of these instances, we would argue that the drink itself is both essential and incidental. Giving drink to the thirsty people in each of these examples is simply a way of saying "I care," "Thank you," or "I love spending time with you." In each case, the drink reveals a thirst to be known by and connected to another person who is willing to take time out of his or her busy day, notice I have needs, and provide for me. It is in these acts of connection that we find the grace that turns this simple task into a spiritual exercise, reminding us that we are truly worthy in God's eyes, and each other's.

Here are some simple ways you can turn giving drink to the thirsty people in your home into a spiritual exercise:

1. Connect

We like to think that we have a strong connection with our spouse and kids, but sometimes we think we're more connected than we actually are. With the smallest children, this disrupted connection is often expressed in silly, irritating ways. Suddenly, we're barraged by a million questions, a million tiny requests, and a million little annoyingly silly "performances." *"Mommy, watch this!" "Daddy, did you see?!?"* Although these displays can try parents' patience, they are simply a child's way of saying, *"I love you mom and dad. Can I have a little more of you, please?"* When we respond promptly, generously, and consistently to these bids for attention, we quench the thirst for connection in our children's hearts.

Few of these bids for attention are more annoying than the tap, tap, tap on the bedroom door in the middle of the night from a child in need of a drink. Of course, children need their sleep — and parents do too! — but the next time your child needs that cup of water in the middle of the night, be mindful of the opportunity for spiritual growth. Check your sternness. Take a breath. Be patient. Be compassionate. Connect. Let your child know how much he or she is worth by giving him or her a few extra minutes of your sleep time. When you do, think about how God, our Father, is always there for us whenever we need him, day or night, and say a small prayer of thanks. If your child is having a hard time falling back to sleep, take a few extra moments of cuddle time.

Together with your child, ask the Blessed Mother, or "Mommy Mary" as she's known in our house, to cuddle and comfort your child both in the moment with you and once you return to your own bed. Use the time to quietly say a decade of the Rosary. You will come to relish the opportunity for a little extra prayer time and your child will come to associate this beautiful prayer with your warm and comfortable presence that helps them rediscover their peace and restfulness.

2. Embrace the Spirituality of Feeding Your Baby

You made me trust in you, even at my mother's breast.

Psalm 22:9 (NIV)

Nursing moms have a special opportunity to experience feeding their hungry infant or toddler as a corporal work of mommy. St. John Paul II asserted in a 1995 address on breast-feeding: "So human and natural is this bond that the Psalms use the image of the infant at its mother's breast as a picture of God's care for man (cf. Ps 22:9). So vital is this interaction between mother and child that my predecessor Pope Pius XII urged Catholic mothers, if at all possible, to nourish their children themselves (cf. Pius XII, *Address to Mothers*, October 26, 1941)."

Of course, Pope Francis has been famously encouraging of nursing mothers, asserting that they should never be ashamed to nurse even in the Sistine Chapel! He related this story in an interview with *La Stampa*:

> There was a young mother behind one of the barriers with a baby that was just a few months old. The child was crying its eyes out as I came past. The mother was caressing it. I said to her: "Madam, I think the child's hungry." "Yes, it's probably time..." she replied. "Please give it something to eat!" I said. She was shy and didn't want to breastfeed in public while the pope was passing. I wish to say the same to humanity: give people something to eat! ("Never Be Afraid of Tenderness," December 12, 2013)

Theologians remind us that nursing moms also have a special connection with the Eucharist. When you nurse, thank God for giving you the opportunity to feed your baby with your body just as God feeds his children with his own body. Although nursing can be tiresome, use that time to look into your baby's eyes and reflect on being as dependent upon God as your child is on you. Remember, as well, those ancient biographies of the saints that asserted how, along with milk, these holy men and women "suckled virtue" from their mother's breasts.

Bottle Feeding: If you are bottle feeding your baby, remember that your little one still needs cuddling and connection at feeding time. Psychologists note that infant feeding is as much about nurturing your child's soul with your presence as it is nourishing their body with formula. Forego propping up baby's bottle or letting your baby have a bottle alone in her crib or car seat even after they would be capable of holding it themselves. Slow down. Minister to your child with your presence at bottle-feeding time by adopting a nursing position, including skin-to-skin contact when possible, and maximize your connection to your child.

3. Create Snack-Time Connections

A lot of families have an afterschool snack time for their children. Consider making this a special time of connection for your children who are not only thirsty for a tasty beverage after a long day of learning but also thirsting for your acknowledgement of their accomplishments. The English have tea in the afternoon to take some time to pause and reflect, and Norwegians consider *koselig* — the regular time they take with family and friends to sit and have coffee or cocoa together in the winter months — the reason they are largely immune to seasonal depression.

Take a tip from our neighbors across the pond. Instead of running around trying to get a few things done while your kids wolf down their snacks, sit down with your children and take that time to connect over a cup of hot cocoa or glass of iced tea. Pray together and thank God for the little successes of the day and the fact that he has brought you all safely back together. This time will not only make dinnertime pleasant and grace-filled by staving off the "hangries" — that is, hungry, angry kids — it will remind your children of their worth in God's eyes, and yours, by taking a few moments to reconnect with them and remind them that they are yours and you are theirs.

4. Be Hospitable

Your family members aren't the only ones thirsting for companionship. Make yours a hospitable home. Invite people over and be sure to have their favorite beverages available. For the longest time, we didn't drink coffee, but most of our friends did, so we always made sure to have a variety of coffees in our home. When the neighbor kids play in our yard, we make sure to invite them in for a cold soft drink in the summer or hot cocoa in the winter. If you coach a children's sports team, take break time to have a cold drink and lead the team in prayer that God will help you look out for one another, glorify him through your sport, and learn to be good sports on and off the field.

These little gestures are simple ways to make those around you feel loved and refreshed by the time they spend with you.

5. Be Mindful of Others

Even today, much of the world does not have access to potable water. You and your children can do something about this tragedy. As a family, discuss the fact that many people around the world struggle to have access to healthy water. Then ask your family to pay attention to how you use water in your home with an eye toward responding to this need. Resolve to take shorter showers. Keep the water turned off until you're done brushing your teeth. Use the shortest cycles reasonable on your dishwasher or washing machine. Limit how much or how often you water your grass. While you do these things, think of those who are desperate for healthy water and pray for them. Then, once a month, donate the savings on your water bill to an organization like Catholic Relief Services that builds wells for needy communities around the world.

Walking the Little Way of the Family

In this chapter, we've looked at a few ways giving drink to the thirsty in your home can become an opportunity to walk the little way of family life and enable one another to grow closer to God. Consider the following questions to help draw more spiritual growth out of giving drink to the thirsty as a corporal work of mommy and daddy.

– QUESTIONS FOR REFLECTION –

- Of the ways listed in this chapter for drawing more meaning out of giving drink to the thirsty in your home or community, what are most meaningful to you?
- How will you carve out some regular time to sit down as a family over a favorite beverage and make time to connect?
- What are your friends' (and your children's friends) favorite beverages? Make a plan to have them on hand for the next time these people come to visit.
- When was the last time you invited your spouse or your kids out for a one-on-one date over a cup of coffee or hot cocoa? Make a date this week. Do your best to put the focus on learning about their feelings, needs, and joys. Ask thoughtful questions and practice the art of being a good listener.

- Ask your children: What ways would you like, as a family, to respond to the needs of those families around the world who don't have ready access to a healthy water supply?

Prayer

Lord Jesus Christ, you give us Living Water that we might never thirst. Help us to use the opportunities we have to give drink to the thirsty people in our home and community as ways to quench others' thirst for connection with us and with you. Help us to cultivate intimacy and fellowship in our homes by creating rituals that allow us to take time for each other throughout the day. Quench our thirst for you and make us sensitive to the ways those around us thirst for love, attention, kindness, and affection. We ask this in Jesus' name. Amen.

CHAPTER FOUR

Shelter the Homeless

"Martha, Martha, you are anxious and worried about many things. There is need of only one thing. Mary has chosen the better part and it will not be taken from her."

Luke 10:41–42

Pope Francis once surprised parents by asking them to become aware of the homeless hidden in plain sight — their own children! He observed that too many children were "orphans within the family" because their parents were too busy to "waste time" with their children and that many parents do not have "the courage and love to spend time with their kids....They do not converse with their children. They do not fulfill their role as educators. They do not set their children a good example with their words, principles, values, those rules of life which they need like bread." Because of this, children, even children in intact families, experience a "feeling of orphanhood that ... is more profound than we think" (General Audience, January 28, 2015).

Giving shelter to the homeless in the little way of family life requires us to go beyond providing the basic necessities of life for those we love, or, for that matter, putting on a good show for our Pinterest followers. It means filling our homes with a powerful sense of love and belonging that provides them a true shelter from the spiritual, emotional, and relational storms of life.

The Book of Sirach counsels parents that our most important task is to raise faithful children (see 16:1-3). As we reveal in *Discovering God Together: The Catholic Guide to Raising Faithful Kids*, research shows that children are more likely to be religiously committed adults *if they experience the Faith as the source of the warmth in their home*. Cultivating this warmth is what sheltering the homeless in the little way of the family is all about. Here are a few important ways you can walk the little way of family life by turning your home into a true shelter.

1. Family Rituals: Sacred Rites of the Domestic Church

A "family ritual" is a regularly scheduled, planned activity that everyone in the family is expected to be a part of. Family meals are one common example of a family ritual, assuming that they happen regularly, that all the members of the family are expected to be there, and that each member does his or her best to make it a positive, enriching experience.

Rituals are the building blocks of a healthy, thriving home. Research demonstrates emphatically that simple family rituals, like mealtimes, game nights, and family prayer, have real power to make families happier and more stable and make family members more emotionally, socially, and spiritually well-adjusted and physically healthier.

Ideally, families will create both daily *and* weekly rituals of connection that enable them to carve out time to work, play, talk, and pray together. This can often require a radical revisioning of the way most people think about spending their time today as opposed to the recent past. As little as a generation or two ago, it was assumed that family life was the place where socialization occurred and where both children and parents developed a sense of purpose, meaning, and values. Children were permitted to participate in extracurricular activities to the degree that they did not infringe too much on family meals, church, and other important family rituals.

These days, most families have fallen prey to the idea that socialization, meaning, purpose, values, direction, and significant relationships are supposed to happen outside the home, while the family home is reduced to a train station where people pass each other on the way to the really important activities. It is this constant busyness that leads to the homelessness and loneliness that many families feel.

Creating rituals that place family life at the center of life is a spiritual exercise that allows your home to be a true shelter. They foster intimacy and compassion, build a loving community, enable joy, and often require sacrifice. Even if it means sacrificing all but the most important extracurricular activities, making the effort to create regular opportunities for your family to work, play, talk, and pray together is a powerful way families can promote a healthier society by encouraging other families to connect through your witness. Family rituals are, in a sense, the sacred rites of the domestic church.

Here are some examples of what this can look like in practice:

Work Rituals

Individual chores are important, but working *together* helps families trust one another, learn important skills from each other, depend on one another, and serve one another directly. Working together builds a sense of community, shared ownership, and gratitude for what God has given us. Likewise, when family work rituals include charitable projects, they help develop a family's sense of Christian mission. Here are some examples of daily and weekly family work rituals.

Daily:

- Prepare meals together, set and clear the table together.
- Each evening, before bed, take fifteen minutes to straighten up public spaces in the house together.

- Help one another sort laundry (and have a sock-ball fight after!).

Weekly:

- Mow and garden together. (And take a minute to praise God for his creation!)
- Clean the garage together.
- Do a household repair together.
- Volunteer at a local charity together.

Write your own ideas here:

Play Rituals

Playing together as a family fosters a sense of joy, team spirit, and connection that glorifies God by helping members experience the communal life God has given them as the gift it is meant to be! Here are some examples of daily and weekly family play rituals:

Daily:

- Play a few hands of a favorite card game together.
- Read aloud to each other for ten to fifteen minutes.
- Have musicians in the family? Create a family band or have some sing-along time.
- Shoot hoops or play catch for fifteen minutes as a family. Play tag as a family.

Weekly:

- Have a weekly, family game night.
- Schedule a family-day activity every Sunday after church.
- Have a family movie night (make the popcorn together in a pot the old-fashioned way and give people a choice of toppings).
- Bake a special family dessert together on Saturdays or feast days.

Write your own ideas here:

Talk Rituals

In his book *The Seven Levels of Intimacy*, Matthew Kelly asserts that different relationships are characterized by people sharing on seven different levels: 1) clichés; 2) facts and events; 3) opinions; 4) hopes and dreams; 5) feelings; 6) fears, faults, and failures; and 7) personal, emotional, and spiritual needs.

In our experience, unless a family is intentional about fostering deeper conversations, family discussions often fail to get beyond the level of clichés ("How was school?" "OK"), facts ("We're having meatloaf for dinner"), or opinions ("I don't like meatloaf!"). Families have to work a little bit to make sharing on the deeper levels of hopes, feelings, fears, and needs seem like a natural and welcome thing.

Family talk rituals enable families to do the work of taking conversations deeper. They are often combined with work, play, or prayer rituals and make these times more meaningful. Here are some examples:

Daily:

• Use discussion cards at dinner to facilitate interesting conversations.

- Pick a "virtue of the day" in the morning and talk over dinner about how each family member practiced that virtue throughout the day.
- Make it a "job" for each family member to be ready to share at dinner one funny thing that happened that day or a joke that the family will enjoy.

Weekly:

- Make a weekly breakfast date with a child.
- Choose a "goal of the week" either for the family or each person, and then discuss any progress made at a nice family dinner at the end of the week.
- Have a family meeting to discuss ways to take better care of one another.
- Take a weekly walk as a family and share how you've encountered God in the blessings and challenges of the week.

Write your own ideas here:

Prayer Rituals

As Father Patrick Peyton, C.S.C., once said, "The family that prays together, stays together." Of course, for this to be true, family prayer must be meaningful. Family prayer time should involve sharing on a level that helps you all feel closer to both God *and* one another. That means that in addition the beautiful formal prayers of the Church, which may certainly anchor your family prayer time, you should cultivate meaningful personal prayers (of thanksgiving, praise, intercessions, and petitions) as well. We discuss the steps to fostering a meaningful prayer life for both families and children in *Discovering God Together: The Catholic Guide to Raising Faithful Kids*, but the following are some simple examples that can inspire your creativity:

Daily:

- Say grace at meals combined with brief prayers of thanksgiving or petition.
- Give a morning blessing to the children.
- Review the Mass readings of the day (and discuss what they mean to each of you).
- Have bedtime prayers that include a short Bible story.

- Pray together before sending the kids to school or before a game or performance.
- Together, say a decade of the Rosary thoughtfully (or the whole thing depending upon the children's maturity level), asking the children to imagine themselves in the position of the person featured in the decade (followed by brief discussion).

Weekly:

- Attend Mass together as a family, and read the readings together beforehand.
- Have family praise time: sing a few praise songs followed by a thoughtful time of prayers of praise and thanksgiving, contrition, intercession, petitions, etc.

Write your own ideas here:

Beyond Rituals

In addition to establishing solid rituals of connection in your domestic church, here are a few more ideas for making your home a true, spiritual shelter.

2. Create a Beautiful Home

Christians encounter God in beauty. That is why, throughout its history, the Catholic Church has built beautiful churches filled with beautiful things and has had its ministers dress in often elaborate and beautiful vestments. With the right spirit, beauty, art, and ornament can be an important part of creating a sacred space that inspires its occupants to deeper communion with God.

Creating a beautiful home begins with the virtue of stewardship — that is, taking care of the things we have. Keeping an orderly home, a clean home, a home where things are put back in their place when people are done with them and things are well maintained, is not about putting on airs. Done with the proper attitude, *housekeeping is a spiritual exercise* enabling family members to reflect on all God has given them, praise him for his generosity, and express their thanks by taking proper care of those blessings. Keeping everyone on board with maintaining your home can be a chore, but make sure to remind one another that your efforts are not about the stuff itself or showing off for the neighbors, but rather to show God your gratitude and praise him with the way you attend to the gifts you've been given.

Beyond maintaining your home, decorating your domestic church can be a spiritual exercise as well. Again, this isn't about turning your house into a museum showcase. Your efforts at interior decorating should not make people afraid to live in your house. The goal is to create a warm, welcoming space that inspires those who enter it to *reflect, relax, and rejoice.* You don't have to be a millionaire to do this well. You can find many lovely things at secondhand stores and estate sales, and you can get plenty of great decorating ideas from the Internet. As long as your intention is to create a hospitable environment where people feel safe, cared for, treasured, and grateful to God for their blessings, it is virtuous to make your home a beautiful place to live.

3. Practice Detachment

Just as important as decorating your domestic
church is practicing a spirit of detachment about
your decorations. Christian detachment doesn't
mean "don't care about stuff." It means always re-
membering that God and people are more important. The things you have, even the treasures you
value, are only good to the degree that the people
in your home are welcome to use them. Yes, certain things might be reserved for special occasions
or put in places of reverence in your home. Just be
careful not to turn the things you have into idols
that are more precious than the people in your
life or use those things to make other people feel
inferior to you.

By all means, exercise good stewardship of
the gifts God has given you, but if accidents happen and something breaks, don't behave as if your
world has ended. If your children accidentally
damage or destroy something, pray for the grace to
remain calm and understanding. Have them clean
up the mess with you. Review the rules of the
house. Apply whatever consequences you must,
but be careful to never communicate that your

little ones could lose your love because of the loss of some thing. God is always merciful no matter how great our sins. Mirror that mercy.

Another way to practice detachment is to donate gently used treasures and household items to charity. This is another reason to carefully maintain the things you have been given so that when you decide to replace them, someone else may continue to get good use out of them. Assuming it is well cared for, chances are anything you donate could be a real blessing to another family who has less than you. The Church asks us to care for the things we have as if we are holding them in trust for the next people who will own them.

4. Create a Prayerful Space

In addition to being a beautiful space, make your home a sacred space. Display meaningful religious art, statuary, and other items around your home. These things are called "sacramentals," a word that means "little mysteries." Such items become part of the backdrop of your home that reminds you of your spiritual destiny: to become part of the Communion of Saints!

Psychologists and spiritual directors both tell us that in order to live authentically we have to remember that every moment of every day — even the boring mundane moments — is potentially packed with divine purpose. Having religious objects around the home helps us remember that we are part of God's family, and they proclaim to those who visit your home that while other families may choose to serve more worldly masters, you and your house will serve the Lord (see Jos 24:15).

In addition to displaying religious objects around your home, it can be a wonderful thing to create prayer spaces — simple altars or displays including things such as a crucifix, a candle, a Bible, and a picture of a favorite saint — that can serve as focal points for personal or family prayer. Children especially love to create these spaces in their rooms. They don't have to be elaborate to be meaningful, and enlisting your children's help to create such spaces encourages your kids in their personal prayer lives. It is not unusual for families who have created such spaces in their homes to find their children spontaneously stopping for a brief moment of prayer and reflection. It is in such moments that parents feel especially blessed to be given the opportunity to be raising a godly family.

5. Remember the Homeless

Regularly talk with your family about what you can do to remember those less fortunate. Is there an organization in your community that builds homes for needy families? Perhaps your family could volunteer to lend a hand together. Remember to turn off your lights and donate your savings to a local homeless shelter. At the very least, adults should keep a few dollars in their front pocket, at the ready, to give to a needy person they may meet. For safety reasons, it would be prudent to let children know that giving money to strangers is something that should be reserved to their parents, but children should at least witness their parents being actively generous. But gently encourage your children to give you a few dollars from their allowance to add to the amount you keep in your pocket to distribute to the poor so that they can be participate in giving alms too.

The Family as Spiritual Powerhouse

Sheltering the homeless while walking the little way of the family means making God a member of your household. Your family should encounter him in the beauty and comfort of your home, in the gratitude you express to him for your blessings, in the way you treat one another, and in the way you share what you have with others. Let your home become the domestic church — a hub of love, beauty, charity, and grace — that it is meant to be.

– QUESTIONS FOR REFLECTION –

- Growing up, did you have family rituals? If so, what did you do and how did those rituals draw your family closer to one another and God? If not, what rituals did you see friends' families or families on television celebrate that you wish your family would do? How can you incorporate these into your family life today?

- With so many things going on, people often struggle to give their families the time they justly require. What small changes could you begin to make this week to start carving out some time for your family to work, play, talk, or pray together a little more?

- "Divide and conquer" is a common motto for families, but this strategy can cause us to miss out on opportunities to create family rituals. Are there some household tasks or other activities people in your home do by themselves but, with a little creativity, could be made into opportunities to work, play, talk, or pray *together*?

- What ways do you use religious art and sacramentals to make your home a prayerful place? What additional things can you do to remind family members that God is present in the little moments of everyday life in your home?

- How does your family care for those less fortunate? What are some simple things your family could do to become more actively attentive to the needs of those who are without adequate housing?

Prayer

Lord Jesus Christ, you reminded Martha of the important difference between taking care of a house and mak-

ing a home. Help us to make our homes truly hospitable, grace-filled places where our families and guests can experience loving communion, respect, mutual service, joy, and all the virtues that enable us to appreciate life as a gift. Give us the grace we need to make our family life a priority and to protect the many ways we work, play, talk, and pray together in the sacred rites of our domestic church. Let our commitment to generously serving one another and our community be a witness and a sign of your love, that you might change the world through our family. Amen.

CHAPTER FIVE

Clothe the Naked

"His son said to him, 'Father, I have sinned against heaven and against you; I no longer deserve to be called your son.' But his father ordered his servants, 'Quickly bring the finest robe and put it on him; put a ring on his finger and sandals on his feet."

Luke 15:21

In the parable of the prodigal son, the father commands that his repentant son be given his own ring, the finest robes, and new sandals as a sign that he has restored his son's dignity. Families spend a lot of time with clothes: buying clothes, figuring out what to wear, washing clothes, putting clothes away. It is easy to forget, but on the little way of the family, the act of dressing ourselves and our children is packed with spiritual significance.

Revealing Who We Are

Christians venerate the body as a holy icon upon which we can find God's own fingerprints. Through our bodies we communicate who we are and what we are meant for. The body isn't just what's on the outside of us. It reveals who we are inside too. As St. John Paul II asserted, "The body, and it alone, reveals that which is invisible, the spiritual and the divine" (General Audience, February 20, 1980).

Clothe the naked as a corporal work of mommy and daddy is not merely about teaching our little ones to cover up in any old thing. It is about teaching our children to carry themselves with the dignity of a son or daughter of God in their outward appearance, in the way they behave, and in the way they relate to others.

Looking a little deeper, we must remember that nakedness isn't just about the body. Nakedness also speaks to the pain we feel when others treat us in a manner that is beneath our dignity and we feel ashamed and vulnerable. That's why St. John Paul taught in his Theology of the Body that the opposite of loving someone is using them.

When we love someone, we remind them of their dignity as a person, as a child of God. But when we *use* someone, we turn them into a *thing*, a tool we can use however we want. Any time someone tries to use us, or we allow ourselves to be used, we feel naked. We want to crawl up into a little ball and hide. Ultimately, then, *clothing the naked* means wrapping each family member in a love that reminds them of their dignity in Christ and helps them know, in their bones, when they are being treated well and when they are being treated poorly.

This might sound odd at first. How could people, especially children, *not* know whether they are being treated well or not? Sadly, our counseling practice is filled with people who have little to no sense of this. Raised in homes where their needs were not responded to promptly, generously, or consistently; where they were neglected, abused, disregarded, or treated at least as an inconvenience if not trash; or where they were taught to see everything as their fault even when it wasn't — these men and women grew up with a gut-level ignorance of what it meant to have their dignity as persons respected. They might know intellectually what love is supposed to look like, but they don't have a living, working experience of it, and their relationships reflect this lack.

By contrast, those children who are raised in households where parents do respond to their children's needs promptly, generously, and consistently, and are treated with respect and taught to treat those around them respectfully in return, have a gut-level sense of what healthy relationships look like. They know how to choose healthy, godly friends and partners who will work for their good, and set limits or withdraw from people who would use them or treat them in a manner that is beneath their dignity. They may or may not be able to define love as a theologian or philosopher would, but they know in their gut what the real thing feels like, and they are better equipped to spot imposters. In this sense, clothing the naked means wrapping our children's souls in an experience of authentic parental and godly love that allows them to discern between the warmth of a healthy relationship and the heat of unhealthy drama.

The following are some ways you can practice both senses of this corporal work of mommy and daddy in your home.

1. Dress Well

You don't have to have a lot of money to dress yourself and your children with dignity and, yes, style. With some careful shopping, you can outfit your family with a beautiful wardrobe at a thrift shop. But if dressing in a manner that is befitting a son or daughter of God doesn't require a lot of money, it does require you to have a sense of your worth as a child of God. Simple isn't the same as sloppy. Modest isn't the same as frumpy. Some well-meaning people mistakenly avoid dressing with dignity and style because they think it would make them appear prideful. But pride is not the sin of thinking well of ourselves. It is the sin of thinking *only* of ourselves. In the Book of Psalms, King David praises God saying, "I am fearfully and wonderfully made" (139:14, NIV). Take a page from David's book and find the courage to rejoice in the beauty God gave you!

In his *Introduction to the Devout Life,* St. Francis de Sales reminds us that we should present "an attractive faith" to the world in the way we dress and act. Doing so says to the people we meet: "Get to know me. I have something valuable to share with you."

When we dress as sons and daughters of God, we make people aware that, by God's grace, we are persons of substance. We do not claim this for ourselves. It is a gift given to us by God, and we glorify him by celebrating it. This is never truer than when we go to Mass, and we should be mindful about how we dress for church. As parents, we love to see our children taking care of the things we have given them. We're glad they are enjoying our gifts, and we are proud that they are being responsible with those gifts. Your heavenly Father has given you the gift of your body, your beauty, and your dignity. When you go to church, show him that you are enjoying and caring for that gift. And don't scowl at people who don't dress as well or as modestly as you think they should. That *would* be prideful. Just bear witness to your own God-given beauty. That will be enough.

2. Remember: People are the Point

Everything we said about stewardship in the last chapter applies to clothing as well. As a family, practice taking care of your clothes as if they have been given to you to be eventually given to others — because they were. Teach children how to care for, wash, and put away their clothes properly. Every few months, have you and your kids go through your closets and donate any gently used items you no longer need to local charitable organizations.

3. Love Well

Of course, how we care for and think about our clothing is only part of it. Clothing the naked in our homes also means loving each other well so that we don't feel exposed, taken advantage of, or taken for granted by each other. Families cover each other in dignity when they respond to one another's needs and requests promptly, generously, and consistently.

Again, this doesn't mean spoiling one another or encouraging selfishness. It means encouraging what St. John Paul called "mutual self-donation."

Self-donation invites us to consider all that we have been given — our time, treasure, talents, and even our bodies — and ask how we might use those things to make the lives of those around us easier or more pleasant. More than any other quality, it is self-donation, that kind of heroic generosity of self, that helps us become saints. When self-donation is *mutual* — that is, it is not just practiced by one person in a family but by everyone in the family — our homes become true "communities of love" where each person's needs are generously met without any one person having to be solely responsible. When self-donation is *not mutual*, a codependent household can result where one person is so concerned with serving the other family members that he or she unintentionally enables everyone around him or her to become more selfish. In such a family, the one with the servant's heart is not seen as a person but a vending machine that dispenses service and can be ignored when its working well and (metaphorically) kicked when it isn't.

To encourage mutual self-donation, take a few moments over dinner or at bedtime to ask what each member of your family might do to make each other's lives easier or more pleasant the next day. Regular conversations such as this remind family members that the goal of family life is learning how to care for one another with the love that comes from God's own heart.

4. "Disciple" Children in Their Relationships

In addition to modeling love in your home, you clothe your children's souls with dignity by having regular conversations with your kids about how they are treated by (and treat) both friends and boy/girlfriends. Parents often feel like trespassers when they ask their children to talk about these relationships, but that is a tragic mistake. Of course, we shouldn't lecture our children or smother them, but we *must* "disciple" our children into healthy, Christian relationships. The most important lesson to convey here is that Christian friendship (including dating) is all about working for each other's good. We should expect our children to raise the bar with their friends, to be the ones suggesting wholesome activities, redirecting inappropriate conversations, standing up for those who might be bullied or ridiculed, and opposing immoral behavior. Dating relationships should especially reflect this dynamic. Again, they don't need us to lecture them, but they will need our ongoing encouragement, support, and guidance, especially if their "friends" try to bully or pressure them into abandoning their dignity. Just remember, the point of discipling our children in their peer relationships is not to be moralistic scolds or killjoys. It is to help our children discover how to have healthy, joyful, godly friendships. Children shouldn't be left out in the cold to figure these things out on their own. Clothe their naked hearts with your loving guidance and example.

5. Model Love in Your Marriage

Few things make children feel more naked and vulnerable than parents who don't get along or aren't openly caring. Christian parents must teach their children the value of saving themselves for marriage, but if we want our children to do this, we parents must present a model of marriage worth saving themselves for. Act lovingly toward your spouse. Even if your kids tease you about it, there is little that makes them feel more secure than seeing that mom and dad really love each other. Likewise, make regular time to keep working on your marriage — even when there aren't problems. Read Catholic books on marriage enrichment, go to marriage retreats, discuss how you and your spouse can take better care of each other, and, if you are having difficulties, get faithful, professional marriage counseling help quickly. Studies show that couples often suffer for four to six years before seeking help. That's a long time to make children feel naked and vulnerable because their parents can't get their lives in order. Clothe your children's naked hearts by modeling the love you want them to have when they grow up.

Clothing the Naked and the Little Way of Family Life

In the little way of family life, the corporal work of mommy and daddy *clothing the naked* helps you remind each other of your dignity as children of God, both in the way you carry yourselves and in the way you relate to each other. Likewise, it enables you to remind the people you encounter throughout the day that they are meant for more and they glorify God when they dress, behave, and relate in a manner befitting their Christian dignity.

– QUESTIONS FOR REFLECTION –

- Are there certain outfits that help you put your best foot forward at work, school, play, and church? What are they? Why do you feel these outfits do such a good job of showing off your dignity as a child of God?

- Does your family work together to treat your clothes as if you were holding them in trust for others to use? How could you do a better job as a family to be good stewards of your clothes?

- Does your family work together to do things to attend to the needs of those who do not have warm or adequate clothing? What could you do as a family to be more mindful of the needy in your community?

- Does your marriage and family life exemplify the kind of love that reminds those in your home of their dignity as children of God and helps everyone feel safe, special, and cared for? What could you do as a family to better attend to one another's dignity and make one another's lives easier or more pleasant?

- Do you have the kind of relationship with your children that makes conversations about their relationships with their peers seem easy and natural? What could you do to make such conversations more common, casual, and productive?

Prayer

Lord God, you reminded us it is your will that we should be dressed more finely than the lilies of the field. Help us to dress in a manner that is reflective of our dignity as your children. Help us to see that those in need are able to dress in a manner that is befitting their dignity as well, and help us always to clothe each other in the love that comes from your heart so that we never feel naked, alone, vulnerable, or used. We ask this through Jesus Christ our Lord. Amen.

CHAPTER SIX

Visit The Sick

Jesus went around to all the towns and villages, teaching in their synagogues, proclaiming the gospel of the kingdom, and curing every disease and illness.

Matthew 9:35

"Mom? Dad? I don't feel so good." Whether you hear those words in the middle of the night, when you are already running late for work, when you are on the phone with school in the middle of an important meeting, or when you finally get that vacation you've been looking forward to all year, they never seem to come at a convenient time. Of course, it's never really convenient to have to deal with a sick child, but why does it have to happen *today of all days?*

We've all been there. And if keeping your cool and finding the wherewithal to be attentive and compassionate when an unexpected illness throws a wrench in your best-laid plans isn't a spiritual exercise — an opportunity to die to ourselves and find a way to be present to another in their time of need — we don't know what is. Here are some things to keep in mind the next time a patient in your house-pital needs a little extra TLC.

1. Be Present

Although it can be a hardship, try to be the one who is home with your child when he or she is ill. Time with mom or dad can be every bit as healing as a trip to the doctor.

Treat sick days as special opportunities to re-connect with your child. Take time to read stories to him or her, play a quiet game, or do a simple art project, as your child's energy level allows. Resist the temptation to park a sick child in front of the television all day or pawn him or her off on a sitter while you try to get stuff done. Of course, when an illness drags on for several days — especially for those parents who are dealing with a chronically ill child — it can be important to get breaks as you can, but for briefer bouts of sickness, try to re-member that God, who has the busiest schedule in the universe, tells us there is nothing more important than making time "for the least" (Mt 25:40).

2. Plan Ahead

We don't even like to think about our kids being sick, but it can be helpful to plan ahead. Plan a "sick-day schedule" in advance. Have the numbers for your alternative caregivers at the ready, just in case, and make a list of some specific examples of the types of activities we mentioned above that you could do with a low-energy and potentially cranky child so that you have one less thing to think about on the days when everything is thrown into chaos. When you are making your sick-day plan, don't just think about how you will manage the various sick-day events and tasks, *focus on what will enable you to be truly present* to your child. Are there certain treats — hot cocoa; a favorite tea; a healthy, special snack — you can keep on hand for just such occasions? Likewise, especially for young children, it can be helpful to have a special sick-day activity basket planned with new coloring books, fresh clay, or a few new stories to keep little ones distracted and less likely to become bored and irritable. When making your plan, take a moment to ask the Blessed Mother to help you think of all the things that would help you bring God's love and her heart to your children through your care.

3. Be Kind

It's easy to give into a spirit of irritation when we have to attend to a sick child. If you begin to feel irritable, take a moment to ask God for the grace to be calm, to be caring, and to be compassionate. Remember that we are the hands and face of Christ to others, especially to our little ones. Parents teach their children how to expect God to care for them by how we attend to them. The degree to which parents respond promptly, generously, and consistently to their children's needs becomes the internal road map that informs children's expectations about how much they can trust others, and how we can expect to be treated by others — including God. God asks moms and dads to be his face to their little ones so that they might experience his compassion through our care. If you feel tension or resentment rising within you, take a breath, pray for an extra measure of grace, put the patience and compassion back in your tone of voice and a smile on your face, and be grateful for the opportunity to show your child God's healing face.

4. Remember Your Spouse

Of course, sometimes moms and dads get sick and require some special, loving care, too. It can be tempting to think that, because they are grown-ups, they ought to just take care of themselves. After all, aren't you busy enough? And all the things they can't do aren't going to resolve themselves.

Although it can be challenging, try to step out of that busy, put-upon feeling and be present to your mate. Do those extra chores cheerfully. Bring your spouse a favorite hot beverage or snack. Offer to sit with him or her awhile when you can. Let your mate rest his or her head in your lap and sit quietly together. Take these special times to pray together for your marriage and for a speedy recovery.

Get your kids to help out as well so they have the opportunity to learn the joy of helping others.

Hopefully, things will get back to normal soon, but in the meantime, take advantage of this corporal work of mercy to grow in selflessness and generosity and help your spouse feel God's love through your care.

6. Don't Spread Illness

It is so frustrating to have to change plans at the last minute. When we or our children become ill, it is so much easier to keep that play date, send the child to school, or go to work, and hope no one will notice. Resist this temptation. If loving others means working for their good, we are definitely not behaving lovingly when we put them at risk for sickness. Put people before plans.

7. Remember Those in Need

Sadly, there are many families with children who have chronic illnesses. Having to face sickness over a long haul can be exhausting and demoralizing. Ask yourselves what you can do to alleviate some of the stress and sadness of these families. If you know such a family, you might volunteer to provide child-care and respite for parents who are desperate for a break. You might also consider putting together an activity basket like the one we mentioned above for a sick child and/or their siblings. If you don't personally know a family who could benefit from such a gift, contact your local children's hospital to see what small things your family can do to bring a little comfort and compassion to a sick child or struggling family.

Of course, children are not the only ones who get sick and need our compassion. If your children are old enough to not feel intimidated by strangers or infirmity, consider contacting a local nursing home to see what volunteer or visiting opportunities may be available. Your presence can make all the difference to such a resident, for whom loneliness can be just as serious an illness as any physical deficit. As a special project, perhaps your children could draw a picture of a resident's patron saint, do a little study on that saint, and present it to that elderly person on your next visit. Regardless, at the very least, in your family's bedtime prayers remind your child to pray for those who are sick and in special need of God's grace.

Visit the Sick and the Little Way of the Family

Visit the sick, the corporal work of mommy and daddy, reminds us that God and his grace are abundantly present even when we and those we love are not feeling the best. In the little way of the family, there will be many opportunities to take advantage of this grace to help us be more patient, loving, and compassionate parents, and to help our children encounter the gentle and healing spirit of God. Likewise, when we remember those who are sick in our community in our family's prayers, we allow God to reach out to the whole world through our family. By embracing the moments of grace that often accompany illness, we can draw closer to God and one another and come one step closer to becoming the saints we are meant to be.

– QUESTIONS FOR REFLECTION –

- Growing up, how did your parents respond to you when you were sick? Did the way they cared for you reveal God's love to you? Why or why not? Is their example one you would like to follow in ministering to the sick in your family?

- What ideas can you think of that would make sick days at home more pleasant and loving? What activities can you plan for these times that would make them more bearable for you and your child?

- When do you tend to become irritable or tense when dealing with your sick child or spouse? How can you approach these situations differently in the future to see them as opportunities for you to grow in grace, compassion, and kindness?

- In what ways does your family keep in mind the sick in your community? Are there any other small things you can do as a family to bring comfort to those around you who may be dealing with illness or infirmity?

Prayer

Lord Jesus Christ, in your mercy, you healed the sick and infirm and brought comfort to all those you encountered. Help our family respond in kindness, mercy, and compassion to those who are sick in our home, extended family, and community. Empower us to be instruments of your healing grace, and help us to embrace the opportunities for growth that come from being compassionate to those who are suffering. We ask this through Christ our Lord. Amen.

CHAPTER SEVEN

Visit the Imprisoned

I form you and set you / as a covenant for the people.... / To say to the prisoners: Come out! / To those in darkness: Show yourselves! / Along the roadways they shall find pasture.

Isaiah 49:8-9

Fathers, do not provoke your children, so that they may not become discouraged.

Colossians 3:21

We don't often think of visiting the imprisoned as a normal part of the little way of family life, but in the little way of the family, this corporal work of mommy and daddy speaks to the heart of how parents practice discipline in the home.

Consider that most people are not held in prisons made of concrete and iron bars but rather prisons made of uncontrolled passions, bad habits, unbridled emotions, and thoughtlessness. Parents who practice this corporal work of mommy and daddy by disciplining with love and grace actually set their children from these influences and teach their children how to live in a manner that glorifies God in all they do. When your little prisoner is "doing time" in the corner chair, on the stoop, or in solitary confinement in his or her room, it is your ability to respond in mercy that will determine whether he or she will display more appropriate and godly behavior in the future or if he or she will exhibit even greater misbehavior out of ignorance or spite.

Saints who ministered to children often offered counsel that gentle discipline is a parent's best hope both for raising godly children and for overcoming the anger, impulsiveness, and hot-temperedness that often makes it difficult for us to be godly disciplinarians. According to St. John Bosco, founder of the Salesian Preventive System of child-rearing, disciplining children is a spiritual exercise that benefits both parents and children. In articulating his approach to discipline, he referenced his own patron saint, St. Francis de Sales. As *The Salesian Bulletin* recounted:

St. Francis de Sales, that meekest of saints, never allowed his tongue to speak when his spirit was disturbed. "I am afraid," he once said, "to lose in a quarter of an hour that little sweetness that I have gathered up, drop by drop, like dew, in the vessel of my heart through the efforts of 20 years." Master your own character, and then you will succeed in mastering those of your [children]. Show them that uncontrolled emotion plays no part in your actions; they will respect you for that, and their respect will prompt their obedience. But betray the least sign of weakness, of passion, of impatience, and your authority and prestige will not long endure. Besides, your punishment will not be taken as a remedy for the boy's fault, but as a vent for your own passion. It can bear no fruit!

Any parent knows that what St. John Bosco proposes is a tall order. Mastering our own characters as parents can seem like a full-time job. And yet, that is exactly what an effective and godly dis-

ciplinarian must do. Godly parents know that being merciful to a misbehaving child doesn't mean
letting that child off the hook, but rather being an
example of self-control, thoughtfulness, kindness,
and wisdom that the child can turn to as both a
model and an inspiration. We discuss how to prac-
tically apply St. John Bosco's insights (and many
others) on discipline in our book *Parenting with
Grace,* but here are a few ways you can begin to
honor the spirit of this corporal work of mommy
and daddy and practice graceful discipline in your
home.

1. Practice Charitable Interpretation

St. Ignatius of Loyola urged Christians to practice
the art of charitable interpretation. That doesn't
mean making excuses for bad behavior. It means
being willing to see people in a merciful light even
when they act in ways that irritate or upset you.

Applied to parenting, this means that Christian
parents try hard not to take their children's behavior as a personal insult or behave as if their children
are trying to be difficult or manipulative — even
when they are. Rather, parents who practice the

art of charitable interpretation work hard to see bad behavior as a flawed attempt to meet a need or a good intention, and they believe it is their job to help their children meet those needs and intentions more appropriately the next time. Practicing charitable interpretation stops parents from feeling like wardens and, instead, enables them to be guides in the art of godly living.

2. Teach the Positive Opposite

Teaching the "positive opposite" means putting more energy into helping kids behave well than yelling at or punishing them for getting it wrong. For instance, if a child expresses his anger disrespectfully, instead of simply yelling, "DON'T YOU DARE TALK TO ME THAT WAY!" a parent teaching the positive opposite might say: "You may not speak like that to me. If you need to let me know that you're upset, please say, 'I feel so angry!' [or some other similar, acceptable phrase]. Now, try that again." The parent will then make the child repeat the more respectful words until the child can use the right words and tone of voice and display an appropriate expression.

When timeouts are needed, don't use them as stand-alone punishments — that rarely works. Instead, use them to give your child an opportunity to calm down enough to really hear what you're saying about dealing with similar situations in the future. Committing to teaching the positive opposite means helping your child discern the right thing to do in a lot of different situations instead of simply yelling at the child for getting it wrong and hoping they'll eventually sort the right answers out on their own.

3. Use Logical Consequences

Parents who are attempting to walk the little way of family life by being merciful disciplinarians will work hard to apply logical consequences that provide a structure for good behavior as opposed to piling on punishments that fail to teach any new skills. For instance, if a child fails to clean his room, either at all or to the parent's standards, simply grounding him for a week probably won't teach him to clean his room nearly as well as saying: "Your room needs to be cleaned to my standards before you may go to baseball practice or your games. If you get done late, you will get to practice or your game late. If you don't do it at all, you won't go at all. It is your choice."

This is just one example. This chapter is not meant to be a comprehensive parenting guide. We merely want to show the different attitude that parenting in the spirit of the corporal works of mommy and daddy requires. Parents who wish to walk this path understand how to use logical consequences to create a structure that encourages good behavior in the short-term, and in the long-term helps the child become a godly person.

4. Teach Virtue

In order to set our children free from bad behavior, we need to actively teach virtuous behavior instead. One technique is to *catch your child being good* by pointing out things they do correctly so they learn that they can please you by behaving rightly. Another is to *choose a "virtue of the day"* that you work on as a family throughout the day, and then discuss your progress on and struggles with it over dinner. Just remember, parenting can only fulfill its potential as an engine of spiritual growth (for parents and children) when parents actively teach children how to be good people, not when they wait for children to misbehave, slap on a punishment, and declare, "Mission accomplished." Virtue is the key to setting people free from the prisons that stop them from fulfilling their godly destiny to become saints.

5. Cultivate Relationship

There is a truism that says, "Rules without rapport equals rebellion." If your child seems to be stuck in a bad attitude or is consistently displaying poor behavior, strengthening your relationship can often be key for a path to success.

It might sound counterintuitive; after all, you're probably feeling pretty irritated with your child and think that you could both benefit from some time apart. The opposite is actually true. The more irritated you are with your child, the more time you actually need together to get back in sync. Getting yourself to the point where you are able to reinvest in your relationship with your misbehaving child can be a tremendous opportunity for spiritual growth.

Ask God for the grace to remember how lovingly he deals with you when you let him down. Then extend that mercy to your child. Take some special one-on-one time with your child. Do something you both enjoy that gives you a little time to talk. Tell your child that you know that you both have had a hard couple of days with each other but you'd like to work things out so that you can put all that behind the two of you. Ask your child what he or she thinks he or she might need to move forward, and share your own ideas. Don't lecture. Don't criticize. Problem solve *with* your child. You might be surprised how, given the chance, even very young children can come up with some very good ideas for getting back on track.

6. Remember Those in Need

While it would probably not be prudent for you and your family to do direct prison ministry together, there are still things you can do to make a difference. See if your diocese or other local charity collects toys or clothing for the children of those who are in prison. Remember to pray for those who are imprisoned that they might experience God's mercy and transforming grace and that their families would know God's providence.

Visiting the Prisoner and the Little Way of Family Life

Christians know that to be truly free we must be able to choose what is good and right. If we must act on every angry impulse, indulge every craving, or feel compelled to act on every want or desire, are we truly free? Of course not. Using gentle, logical approaches to disciplining our children gives them the ability to choose the right path — not because they are being forced to do so, but because we have helped set them free to see and choose the best response to any situation. Choosing this kind of thoughtful, intentional, graceful approach to discipline over other more reactive, emotional approaches requires parents to not only teach but also learn from those times when they have to correct their children. This process can be a powerful spiritual exercise that enables both parents and children to grow in self-mastery, emotional control, wisdom, and empathy. For more information on how to employ more graceful approaches to discipline in your home, please see *Parenting with Grace: The Catholic Parents' Guide to Raising (almost) Perfect Kids.*

– QUESTIONS FOR REFLECTION –

- When you have to correct your child, do you usually teach "the positive opposite," or do you tend to simply impose punishments or consequences? Regardless, what more could you do to help your child choose to do the right thing as opposed to simply avoiding the wrong thing?

- How could you change your approach to discipline so that it is more about teaching virtue than about correcting or punishing wrongdoing?

- When are you most tempted to lose your temper or yell at your children for wrongdoing? How will you learn to control your temper in these situations so that you can model the self-control your want your children to exhibit?

• In addition to administering appropriate corrections, what do you do or could you do to strengthen your relationship during those times when your child is exhibiting consistently poor behavior or attitudes?

Prayer

Lord Jesus Christ, even though we are completely undeserving, you constantly extend mercy to us and deal with us gently when we fail you. We praise you for your generosity and ask you for the grace to extend your generous mercy to our children. Help us to control our own reactions — driven by hurt, anger, or frustration — and, instead, respond to our misbehaving children in love and with wisdom so that we might teach them in the ways they should go and give them the tools they need to glorify you in all their actions. Set us and our children free to choose what is right and serve you in all that we do, that your glory might shine out in our lives. We ask this in the name of Jesus Christ our Lord. Amen.

CHAPTER EIGHT

Bury the Dead

"Blessed are they who mourn, for they will be comforted."

Matthew 5:4

Life is filled with endings, and parents must prepare children to deal gracefully with these endings. Whether those endings involve the loss of a family member, the death of a pet, a broken heart, the loss of friends, or dealing with upheaval in the family, we learn to bury the dead both literally and figuratively when we help our children manage these losses and transitions in faithful, hopeful ways. Here are some things to keep in mind to help your children deal with death and loss gracefully.

1. Remember What We Were Made for
Because we know that death is not the end, Christians sometimes feel guilty about being sad when

we lose a loved one. We should never feel guilty for this. Yes, we have the hope of heaven for those who die in God's grace, but the truth is *we were not made for death.*

St. Thomas Aquinas taught that death is an "unnatural separation" of body and soul. We were never meant to live without one or the other. Although heaven awaits those who die in God's grace, death itself is a grave injustice. We are right to be sad about it. If you or your children are sad about a loss, don't try to pretend otherwise. It can be unbearably difficult to see our children sad, but don't let that discomfort cause you to do further violence to your children by preventing them from having or expressing their feelings. Just hold them. Be honest with them. Let them know that you are sad too, but it will be okay because God loves you and because you will love each other through the sadness and back to joy again.

2. Take Some Time Together

Children who are grieving any kind of loss at any age need "time-in" with you. Regardless of the nature of the loss, be sure to take a little extra time to be together. Slow down. Take some time off work or school so you can strengthen your connection as a family. Hug more. Cuddle together. Sit and be still together. The ministry of presence is the greatest gift we can give a person who is suffering with a loss. This goes double for our children. Don't worry about what to say. Remind them through your physical presence that you are here with each other and for each other through this sad time. The right words will come if you can first connect in a more honest and heartfelt way with each other.

3. Grieving Is about Connecting, Not Letting Go

Grieving is not about letting go. It is about finding healthy ways to stay connected to what was lost. In helping your children deal with the loss of a beloved relative, for instance, think of how you might be able to hold on to the lessons you learned from that person or the experiences you shared. Perhaps you and your younger child could draw pictures of the best times you had with that loved one. With an older child, take time to write out your favorite memories or things you learned about life, yourself, God, or love because of your relationship with that person. Find and display pictures and talk about the memories associated with them. Don't ever pretend a loss didn't happen or that grief is too private to be shared. The best way to shelter your child is to walk with your child through the grief and toward the healing.

4. Be Open

Children tend to do best with sad things if those things can be kept in the open where our children can see them. Often, in trying to shelter our children from death, loss, or other sad events, we hurt them more by leaving them to their imaginations. The stories kids make up inside their heads are usually one hundred times worse than reality.

Of course, our children don't need to know every aspect of a loved one's struggle with terminal illness, or all the concerns we have when we are going through a job loss or other serious family difficulty, but they do need to know something, and they need to know — *in their experience* more than just because you have said so — that it is okay to ask you questions and talk about their feelings, whatever they may be. They can't do that if you are pretending nothing is wrong even though they know something is. Parents often kid themselves thinking that children are oblivious. Children may not attend to all the details, but they are very sensitive barometers to family stress. They know a lot more than you think they do. Yes, it is best to save the serious, heart-wrenching discussions for the supportive adults in your life, but having regular, simple, open, child-friendly conversations about how you are dealing with the loss — including simple conversations about your struggles — can be very freeing and healing to your children. Just remind them that no matter what, they can count on you to be there for them and take care of things. They are certainly entitled to whatever feelings they may have, but one thing they don't have to do is worry that they have to figure things out on their own. That's what mom and dad are meant to be for.

When you are dealing with sadness, like from a death or a divorce, that has certain traditions or rituals associated with it — for example, a funeral, court appearances — it can be helpful to sit down with your child and describe in simple language what the event will be like. Even if they ultimately choose not to go or their presence isn't required, it is better for children if these simple details come from you rather than someone else or your child's imagination. Walking your child through the process ahead of time as well as sharing some comments on how he or she will be expected to behave can be very helpful to a child who really doesn't know what to make of the situation.

5. Be Sensitive

Of course, even after all this, your child might prefer not to attend that funeral or whatever events accompany the particular loss you are going through. If so, don't force him or her to go. Give your child a choice. But whether or not he or she prefers to go, do share — in simple, child-friendly ways — what happened at those events and how those experiences have helped you deal with your feelings about your loss.

Likewise, if your child is dealing with the loss of a pet, be sensitive even if you weren't that pet's biggest fan or if the pet, because it was a bug or some such creature, seemed disposable to you. Take the time to have a respectful burial, draw pictures of favorite memories shared with that pet, and say a prayer asking God to "please take care of _____ and let him be happy with you."

Children often ask if their pets are in heaven. Although the *Catechism* tells us that human beings are the only creation God intended for himself, there are many things we don't know about how heaven "works." It is best to avoid overly detailed responses to this question. Instead, simply tell your child that Christians believe that heaven will contain everything that we need to be happy with God forever. Reassure your child that if he or she needs his or her pet in order to be happy in heaven, that God, in his mercy, would most certainly see to it.

6. Pray

When a family is going through grief or loss, it can be difficult to remember to pray. Sometimes we just forget. Other times we feel too sad or angry with God. That's okay. Tell God these things. Invite your children to be honest with God as well. No, family prayer time is not usually the best time for intense wailing and gnashing of teeth. But family prayer should be honest. Let your children know that God wants to know each of you for real. Bring your grieving, angry hearts to him and give him the chance to take away the pain and fill up that space with his peace and healing.

7. Remember

When your family is going through grief and hard times, it can be easy to feel like it will never end. Intentionally tell stories, and invite your kids to do the same, about times when your family has made it through hardship in the past. Remember how God delivered you. Take time to praise God for his faithfulness in past trials and confidently thank him for the grace he is giving you to get through these present difficulties. Encourage each other to remember how you have pulled together in the past, and offer God the praises he is due as your champion and fortress (see Ps 118:7-9).

Burying the Dead and the Little Way of Family Life

Although it is not a pleasant task, helping our children deal with grief and loss in a hopeful, graceful manner is an important life skill. It is important to teach our children how to bury the dead, literally and figuratively, by facing endings well. In doing so, we remind ourselves that those who live in Christ have nothing to fear and that God always provides for our needs, even in loss. The recommendations in this chapter can help you cultivate a hopeful, resilient spirit in your children and make your family life the safe place you and your children need to heal from the hurt.

– QUESTIONS FOR REFLECTION –

- Did you experience loss or grief as a child? What do you think about the way your parents handled your experience? What would you repeat or change about that approach with your children?

- What do you think would be the hardest part of helping your child cope with grief or loss?

How would you work through these challenges to be truly present to your child?

- How has God brought your family through difficult times in the past? What did you do to pull together? What did you do to draw closer to God? What would you need to do better or differently this time to use this experience to connect with God and one another?

Prayer

Lord Jesus Christ, we praise you even in times of grief and loss because you sustain us even when we are at our weakest. You raise us up and grant us the ability to draw closer to you in times of trial. Help us to respond to our grief and loss gracefully. Enable us to support one another and encourage one another to focus on the resurrection that comes after the cross. We ask this in the name of Jesus. Amen.

CHAPTER NINE

Living the Little Way of the Family

Family life is full of opportunities for profound spiritual growth. Most of us will not do "great" things. We will not lead nations to Christ, or start religious orders that will last centuries, or save lives, or anything like that. But it doesn't matter. As St. Thérèse of Lisieux reminds us, God only asks us to do little things with great love.

The greatest thing we could ever do is introduce our children to God and give them an example of how to love him and follow him with all our hearts, souls, minds, and strength. That is enough, and, fortunately, there are plenty of opportunities to do this in the everyday life of your home.

In the course of our work, we encounter many people who pick on themselves because they "don't do anything" for the Church or the community because they are just "too busy with the family." Of course we are called to do what we can for those suffering outside our door, but if we are not truly and gracefully present to those inside our own four walls, who will be there for them? Who will feed them? Who will shelter them? Who will give them drink, clothe them, nurse them when they are sick, guide them in making godly choices, or teach them their dignity as children of God if not us? And this is no small thing. In fact, the world would be a much better place if every parent gave more time and energy to these activities.

The time we give to our families is not wasted. It is blessed. Every moment, especially the hard, tedious, mundane, frustrating moments, is packed with divine purpose. Don't ever doubt your importance in building the kingdom of God. Raising loving, faithful, joyful, generous children is the single most important key to raising up a loving, faithful, joyful, generous society. Let God fill your heart with his grace. Let God set your family ablaze with the fire of his love. Let God change the world through the imperfect but faithful witness of your family life. Don't just pray as a family. Let your family life BE your prayer. By intentionally asking your family what you can do to better live out the corporal works of mommy and daddy

each day, you will have ample opportunities to become the saints you are called to be. You will be
walking the little way of the family, following the
road that leads you and your loved ones directly to
the loving and merciful heart of God.

Other Books by
Dr. Greg and Lisa Popcak

Parenting with Grace, 2nd Edition

Provides practical advice through a
combination of orthodox theology
with contemporary psychology
along with plenty of good humor.

ID# T964

For Better FOREVER,
Revised and Expanded

The book that has helped couples all over
the world discover new joy, intimacy, and
satisfaction in their marriage is now revised
and expanded. Learn the way to achieve
"happily ever after" by integrating cutting-
edge psychology with a clear articulation of
the Catholic vision of love and marriage.

ID# T1691